Bible Studies

THREE GIFTS, ONE CHRIST

CONVERGE
Bible Studies

THREE GIFTS, ONE CHRIST

KATIE Z. DAWSON

Abingdon Press

Nashville

THREE GIFTS, ONE CHRIST
CONVERGE BIBLE STUDIES

By Katie Z. Dawson

Library of Congress Cataloging-in-Publication Data has been requested.

ISBN: 978-1-4267-7827-8

Series Editor: Shane Raynor

13 14 15 16 17 18 19 20 21 22—10 9 8 7 6 5 4 3 2 1

Manufactured in the United States of America

CONTENTS

ABOUT THE SERIES

Converge is a series of topical Bible studies based on the Common English Bible translation. Each title in the *Converge* series consists of four studies based around a common topic or theme. *Converge* brings together a unique group of writers from different backgrounds, traditions, and age groups.

HOW TO USE THESE STUDIES

Converge Bible studies can be used by small groups, classes, or individuals. Each study uses a simple format. For the convenience of the reader, the primary Scripture passages are included. In Insight and Ideas, the author of the study guide explores each Scripture passage, going deeper into the text and helping readers understand how the Scripture connects with the theme of the study. Questions are designed to encourage both personal reflection and group conversation. Some questions may not have simple answers. That's part of what makes studying the Bible so exciting.

Although Bible passages are included with each session, study participants may find it useful to have personal Bibles on hand for referencing other Scriptures. Converge studies are designed for use with the Common English Bible; but they work well with any modern, reliable translation.

ONLINE EXTRAS

Converge studies are available in both print and digital formats. Each title in the series has additional components that are available online, including companion articles, blog posts, extra questions, sermon ideas, and podcasts.

To access the companion materials, visit

http://www.MinistryMatters.com/Converge

Thanks for using *Converge*!

INTRODUCTION

I was walking through the farmer's market one morning in Des Moines, Iowa, enjoying the smells of fresh-baked goods and the colorful displays of fruits and vegetables. A banjo group was plucking away, and children were rushing by with balloons and face paint. I had a gooey, warm, freshly baked pecan roll and was mid-bite when a voice called out.

"Are you saved?"

Standing on a milk crate, a man was asking everyone and no one this singular question. Some stopped to answer. Others waved him off. The atheists had a booth set up on the opposite corner and seemed to pay no attention. "Are you saved?" he kept calling out, handing a bright yellow pamphlet to anyone who came near. It appears to be a simple, yes-or-no sort of question. But as I stood there in the middle of the street, I realized just how complicated it is.

What do we even mean by the word *saved*?

The origins of the words *save* and *salvation* are a Greek word: *sozo*. Among other things, *sozo* shows up in Scriptures as *to rescue, to deliver, to save someone suffering from death or disease, to heal,* or *to preserve.*

The disciples call out for Jesus to rescue them when their boat is sinking (Matthew 8:25). The hemorrhaging woman touches Jesus' garment and is healed (Luke 8:48). Jesus teaches that deliverance and safety are found by those who seek him (John 10:4-14). Those who believe in the good news are being saved (1 Corinthians 1:18-21).

When have you experienced healing? Do you need to be forgiven or to forgive? Have you been rescued? Did you hear the good news? What strengthened you to keep going? Too often, we reduce the gift of salvation to a yes-or-no question and minimize the life, death, and resurrection of Jesus to a moment on a cross. In doing so, we miss out on the riches of the gifts of salvation that our Savior wants to place in our hands. Even the phrasing of the question "Are you saved?" puts the focus on a moment in the past that we can pinpoint and wrap up with a bow.

I don't know about you, but every day I need strength. I need to hear again and again some good news. I have friends who need healing, and I struggle with forgiveness. I need salvation on a continuous basis. Maybe that is why Paul wrote, "The message of the cross is foolishness to those who are being destroyed. But it is the power of God for those of us who are *being* saved" (1 Corinthians 1:18, emphasis added). Yes, I have already come to know salvation; but I'm also being saved every day. And I'm waiting for that day when I will fully experience the saving power of Jesus Christ. Already, not yet. Jesus came to bring salvation and he is coming again to complete it. The past and the future all colliding together.

The four weeks before Christmas are a time of mental gymnastics in the church calendar. *Advent,* meaning "to come," is a season that intertwines the longing of the prophets for a messiah, the coming of our savior Jesus Christ, and the reminder that his work is not yet finished. Christ will come again. It is a time when we celebrate hope, peace, joy, and love. It is a time when we get to think about salvation in all of its meanings. As we drag out the Christmas decorations and get caught up in the spirit of consumer frenzy, we can be so focused the shiny bows and glittery paper that we forget all about our need for salvation.

We hide our grief for loved ones who have passed and the frustrations of work by filling our bellies and emptying our pockets. We rehearse the spirit of Christmas with strings of lights and fail to see the Light of God shining bright. We give and receive a lot of gifts this time of year, but how often do we spend time exploring the greatest gift of them all? Over the next few weeks, we are going to use the book of Hebrews as our road map, and some unlikely strangers from the east as our tour guides.

Hebrews makes a fantastic guide for this journey because it helps us understand not only who Christ is, but also how we should respond to the amazing gifts of God. And the magi will show us how Jesus becomes our priest, prophet, and king. You see, even though they really don't belong in our nativity scenes, the magi were some of the first to understand the importance of the child born in the stable and placed manger.

As Matthew tells the story, the magi followed a star in the sky—a light in the midst of the darkness—in order to find him. They brought with them three gifts: not random offerings, not treasures from their own lands, but gifts that symbolize who this small child would become.

Gold: a gift for a powerful king.

Frankincense: the symbol of a holy priest.

Myrrh: an oil for embalming the dead.

More than about what the magi give the child, this study is about what Jesus offers us. He comes as the high priest who sacrifices himself for us, the prophet who calls us into a new way of life, and the king of kings who triumphs over evil and sets us free. We will start by setting the stage for the birth of Christ and what makes any of us worthy for the gift of salvation. In the remaining chapters, we will discuss those gifts of salvation represented by the magi. Each chapter will describe a different aspect of what Jesus has done for us and how we can accept God's joy, peace, and love by putting our lives into Jesus' hands.

My prayer is that we will discover a gift that will sustain us long after the wreaths have come off the doors.

1

UNWORTHY
THERE'S A LIGHT IN THE DARKNESS

SCRIPTURE
LUKE 2:7-11; MATTHEW 2:1-2; HEBREWS 2:5-18

LUKE 2:7-11

[7]She gave birth to her firstborn child, a son, wrapped him snugly, and laid him in a manger, because there was no place for them in the guestroom.

[8]Nearby shepherds were living in the fields, guarding their sheep at night. [9]The Lord's angel stood before them, the Lord's glory shone around them, and they were terrified.

[10]The angel said, "Don't be afraid! Look! I bring good news to you—wonderful, joyous news for all people. [11]Your savior is born today in David's city. He is Christ the Lord.

MATTHEW 2:1-2

¹After Jesus was born in Bethlehem in the territory of Judea during the rule of King Herod, magi came from the east to Jerusalem. ²They asked, "Where is the newborn king of the Jews? We've seen his star in the east, and we've come to honor him."

HEBREWS 2:5-18

⁵God didn't put the world that is coming (the world we are talking about) under the angels' control. ⁶Instead, someone declared somewhere,

> *What is humanity*
>   *that you think about them?*
>   *Or what are the human beings*
>   *that you care about them?*
> *⁷For a while you made them lower*
>   *than angels.*
>   *You crowned the human beings*
>   *with glory and honor.*
> *⁸You put everything*
>   *under their control.*[a]

When he puts everything under their control, he doesn't leave anything out of control. But right now, we don't see everything under their control yet. ⁹However, we do see the one who was made lower in order than the angels for a little while—it's Jesus! He's the one who is now crowned with glory and honor because

---

a Psalm 8:4-6

of the suffering of his death. He suffered death so that he could taste death for everyone through God's grace.

¹⁰It was appropriate for God, for whom and through whom everything exists, to use experiences of suffering to make perfect the pioneer of salvation. This salvation belongs to many sons and daughters whom he's leading to glory. ¹¹This is because the one who makes people holy and the people who are being made holy all come from one source. That is why Jesus isn't ashamed to call them brothers and sisters when he says,

> ¹²*I will publicly announce your name*
> * to my brothers and sisters.*
> * I will praise you in the middle*
> *   of the assembly.*[b]
> ¹³He also says,
> *I will rely on him.*[c]
> And also,
> *Here I am with the children*
> * whom God has given to me.*[d]

¹⁴Therefore, since the children share in flesh and blood, he also shared the same things in the same way. He did this to destroy the one who holds the power over death—the devil—by dying. ¹⁵He set free those who were held in slavery their entire lives by their fear of death. ¹⁶Of course, he isn't trying to help angels, but rather he's helping Abraham's descendants. ¹⁷Therefore, he had

---

b Psalm 22:22
c Isaiah 8:17 LXX
d Isaiah 8:18

to be made like his brothers and sisters in every way. This was so that he could become a merciful and faithful high priest in things relating to God, in order to wipe away the sins of the people. [18]He's able to help those who are being tempted, since he himself experienced suffering when he was tempted.

INSIGHT AND IDEAS

In seminary, I spent one summer as a hospital chaplain. I worked mainly on the floor where patients had compromised immune systems because of transplants, leukemia, cancer, or other diseases. Many patients stayed in this wing for weeks at a time; and I had lots of conversations while wearing a paper gown, an isolation mask, and rubber gloves.

One patient, in particular, Adam, was having a hard time. Adam had leukemia and was in a really deep hole of doubt and self-pity. His illness was getting the best of him. I will never forget how, as I entered his room, the first words out of his mouth were, "Why can't I just die already?"

We started talking, but I didn't know what kind of comfort I could bring him. I couldn't take his pain away. I asked whether he wanted to pray; and he barely lifted his head as he answered: "Even if I do admit that God's really there, I don't deserve it."

Adam felt forsaken by God. Forgotten. Hopeless. Unworthy.

Over and over in ministry, folks like Adam have come into my life. They think that grace and faith and salvation are wonderful but believe that they are too far gone, too broken, too messed up to experience it.

But God didn't see Adam, and doesn't see us, as disposable—made, then broken, and easily thrown away. God created each of us, as the psalmist writes, "only slightly less than divine, crowning [us] with glory and grandeur" (Psalm 8:5).

I told Adam that it doesn't matter whether we feel unworthy. It doesn't matter whether we think we are undeserving. The truth is, we are all unworthy and we are all undeserving. There is *nothing* we can do to earn God's love. God created you with glory and honor. And in spite of how you have lived out your life, God loves you anyway.

We are not disposable in God's eyes; we are redeemable. As John 3:16 reminds us, "God so loved the world that he gave" Jesus Christ to save it. God doesn't abandon this creation but, with love and grace, restores it to glory.

OUT OF CONTROL

Growing up, I was fascinated with the sky. Long before there were apps to help pick out the constellations, I created my own star finder, using transparency sheets and glow-in-the-dark puff paint. I mapped out the stars and then held up my faintly shining map to find its match in the heavens.

One of the first constellations I mastered was the Big Dipper, which actually isn't a constellation at all. The stars are part of the constellation Ursa Major. Together these stars make an asterism, or an easily recognizable pattern in the sky.

Those stars, circling overhead, really put into perspective how tiny we are; yet God has put us in control. Our reading from Hebrews quotes Psalm 8, reminding us that God placed this glorious world in our hands for safekeeping.

We have control over how we treat one another. We have control over our children and the animals that surround us. We have even harnessed this world's natural resources for power. But Hebrews takes that gift a step farther. Not only this world, but also the world to come, the world of salvation, has been put under our control. It wasn't given to the angels but to us (Hebrews 2:5, 8).

"Carry out your own salvation with fear and trembling," Paul writes (Philippians 2:12b). It is in our hands. Kind of scary, isn't it?

Maybe that's because, while God may have put everything in our control, we know that sometimes power spins out of control and we hurt one another. Natural disasters such as earthquakes and floods ravage. Violence fills our news stories as neighbors fight and wars rage. We make mistakes. Health declines. Bills pile up. Control? Well, it slips between our fingertips.

My patient Adam was without hope of ever finding that control again. First, he was fighting a disease that could take his life; and he was losing. He was stuck, a prisoner in a body that was betraying him, in a hospital room he had been in for too long.

Second, he had a lot of time to think about the mistakes he had made—too much drinking, too little caring. Even though his disease wasn't caused by his past, he thought that he was being punished for how he had wasted his life. He didn't know how to make amends.

Finally, even if he had decided to take responsibility for his relationships, his health, his faith, everything was a mess. He didn't even know where to start picking up the pieces. He wasn't sure that it was possible.

Maybe you have felt out of control when a disease or disaster turned your life upside-down.

Maybe you have struggled with forgiveness, either of yourself or of someone who has harmed you.

Maybe you have tried to follow Jesus but turned back because the path was too hard.

Maybe you have experienced doubt or despair. Maybe you have been hopeless.

But even in the darkness, we can get our bearings.

A GUIDING STAR

The Big Dipper has been used for centuries to find Polaris, the North Star, to navigate by night. A time-lapse image or video of the northern sky would show countless stars swirling and moving and changing, but Polaris stays a fixed point. The two outer stars in the Big Dipper form an imaginary line that always points to Polaris. And if you are anywhere north of 35 degrees latitude, you can see these stars any hour of the night every day of the year. While the sky may change throughout the seasons and even through the night, Polaris remains still above the horizon.

The author of Hebrews writes that even if we can't see the order, even if this world and the next might appear to be spinning out of control, we need only to find that one star to guide our way; we need only to glimpse Jesus to be reminded that all is not lost (Hebrews 2:9).

The season of Advent is a time when we remember how "the light of God's glory and the imprint of God's being" (Hebrews 1:3) came into this world. Generations of our ancestors longed for the day when they could "walk by the Lord's light" (Isaiah 2:5), when the guiding light, the path of salvation, the end of oppression would be among them.

Matthew tells of the light of God entering the world through the birth of Jesus Christ—a light that shone so bright that it appeared as a star in the sky. It beckoned the magi over mountains and deserts and seas to the countryside of Jerusalem. When they arrived, Jesus may have been a small child in his mother's arms; but that light was so powerful that no darkness could overcome it. That light remains constant, fixed, and always present in this world that is ever changing. He brought light to a world of sin and death.

Jesus is our reference point. He is our North Star. He guides our path to salvation.

DIRTY COVERALLS AND SMELLY SHEPHERDS

Christmas at my Babi and Deda's farm (my grandparents, in Czech) was full of chaos: five children, four spouses, and ten grandkids—all crowded together in their living room, with a gigantic tree in the corner. It was warm and full of joy and laughter, but let's just say that our Christmas scene was unlikely to appear in a Martha Stewart publication.

Instead of wearing Christmas sweaters and pretty dresses, we showed up in wet clothes from sledding and dirty coveralls from feeding the cows. We didn't spend money on silver bows and wrapping paper; our gifts were packaged in grocery bags, newspaper, or sometimes just had tube socks tied around the handle.

When dinner was served, everyone took his or her plate of food and found a chair or spot on the floor to sit. Every inch of the table was covered with the potluck offerings, and there weren't enough chairs anyway.

Rather than singing Christmas carols, we plotted to have the best Christmas prank of the year. The best—or worst— of them all was the dead opossum that was wrapped up and put under the tree. Mind you, it was frozen solid; so it didn't smell.

We were gathered together to celebrate the birth of Christ, but the wrappings of Christmas mattered too. The way our Christmas was packaged, I knew that I could always be myself. I came to believe that there was always room for another person somewhere in the house. Giving mattered more than receiving. We celebrated each person's offering—whether it was of food or story, service, gift, or prank. It was rowdy, disorganized, and a lot of fun.

The story we tell during Advent is as much about the packaging (the setting and the characters) as it is about salvation and Jesus Christ. Of course, the message is important; but how the message is told matters as well. In fact, the surprising way this story played out is one of the reasons it was hard for so many to understand.

God chooses an unwed girl to bear Jesus Christ into the world. His birth takes place in a dark and dirty place, surrounded by animals rather than in the warmth of a bed. The good news of salvation comes to those on the fringes—strangers from afar and lowly shepherds. These details matter. Each person, each place has import. They frame the story so that we won't mistake the fact that this message is for the meek and lowly, the broken and hopeless.

In Luke's gospel, the first to hear the good news about the birth of this savior aren't kings or merchants or religious leaders, but shepherds. Shepherds probably would have felt right at home at Christmas dinner at Babi and Deda's house; but in their day and time they were the unclean, the outcast, and the forgotten. Those whom the rest of the world might consider unworthy are the very ones God chooses.

God is reaching out to the least and the last and the lost, saying: This message is for you. It is good news, "wonderful, joyous news for *all* people" (Luke 2:10, emphasis added).

Every single last one of you. And the message is simple: You are not trapped by sin and death, you are not broken beyond repair, and you are called to participate in the riches of God's glory. Salvation, healing, wholeness, joy, freedom, hope are real, and they are for you.

We might believe that we are unworthy—and we are right.

But we are children of God, and our Creator does not abandon this glorious creation—no matter how tarnished we might have become.

Adam and I had many conversations over that summer. I watched as he let into his life people who showed him love, grace, and forgiveness. I watched as his community rallied in support and helped pay for his treatment. I watched his kids visit, wearing those funny paper gowns and giving kisses through isolation masks. I watched as he navigated this difficult journey with Jesus by his side.

When Adam went home from the hospital, he was learning to accept the gifts that Jesus was bringing into his life. He was set free from a fear of his disease, found forgiveness from the mistakes of his past, and was learning how to put one foot in front of the other on the path of discipleship.

Adam discovered that we are worthy not because of who we are but because of who God is.

God created us with glory and honor. And when God saw us tarnished and bruised, God didn't abandon us but sent Jesus Christ to destroy the power of death, to wipe away the sins of the people, and to help those who are being tempted (Hebrews 2:12-18). Jesus fully entered our human experience so that he might redeem us, heal us, and restore us to the glory and honor God intends for our lives.

As Hebrews 2:11 reminds us: "This is because the one who makes people holy and the people who are being made holy all come from one source. . . . Jesus isn't ashamed to call [us] brothers and sisters."

Isn't that amazing? No matter how messed up and out of control our lives might be, no matter how many mistakes we have made and bridges we have burned, Jesus isn't ashamed of us. He takes our sin and chaos and mess right through the cross. And now he is leading us—the unworthy, broken down, and outcast—straight toward salvation (Hebrews 2:10).

QUESTIONS

1. What is the significance of the Bible's details of the humble circumstances surrounding the birth of Christ?

2. What specifically terrified the shepherds in Luke 2:9? Why might the shepherds have been chosen for the angel to appear to?

3. Who were the magi? Why, do you think, did God decide to notify outsiders about the birth of Jesus?

4. Compare and contrast humans and angels, based on your understanding and the Hebrews 2 passage. In what ways do humans seem to be above the angels? In what ways do we seem to be below them?

5. How is Jesus the "pioneer of salvation" (Hebrews 2:10)?

6. What does it mean to be "made holy" (Hebrews 2:11)? What role, if any, do we play in our being made holy?

7. What do we have in common with Christ (Hebrews 2:14)? Why is this important? How does this factor into the ultimate destruction of the devil by Jesus?

8. How does Christ set us free (Hebrews 2:15)? From what are we being set free?

9. When have you felt out of control of your life? What do you find most difficult about living a life of faith?

10. The Christmas story is a story of hope. Why is hope important? How can we read this story with hopeful expectation and apply it to our own lives?

2

GOLD
A GIFT FOR A KING

SCRIPTURE
ISAIAH 11:1-10; MATTHEW 2:1-21

ISAIAH 11:1-10

¹A shoot will grow up from the stump of Jesse;

　a branch will sprout from his roots.

²The LORD's spirit will rest upon him,

　a spirit of wisdom and understanding,

　a spirit of planning and strength,

　a spirit of knowledge and fear of the LORD.

³He will delight in fearing the LORD.

　He won't judge by appearances,

　nor decide by hearsay.

⁴He will judge the needy with righteousness,

　and decide with equity for those who suffer in the land.

　He will strike the violent with the rod of his mouth;

by the breath of his lips he will kill the wicked.

⁵Righteousness will be the belt around his hips,

and faithfulness the belt around his waist.

⁶The wolf will live with the lamb,

and the leopard will lie down with the young goat;

the calf and the young lion will feed together,

and a little child will lead them.

⁷The cow and the bear will graze.

Their young will lie down together,

and a lion will eat straw like an ox.

⁸A nursing child will play over the snake's hole;

toddlers will reach right over the serpent's den.

⁹They won't harm or destroy anywhere on my holy mountain.

The earth will surely be filled with the knowledge of the Lord,

just as the water covers the sea.

¹⁰On that day, the root of Jesse will stand as a signal to the peoples.

The nations will seek him out, and his dwelling will be glorious.

MATTHEW 2:1-21

¹After Jesus was born in Bethlehem in the territory of Judea during the rule of King Herod, magi came from the east to Jerusalem. ²They asked, "Where is the newborn king of the Jews? We've seen his star in the east, and we've come to honor him."

³When King Herod heard this, he was troubled, and everyone in Jerusalem was troubled with him. ⁴He gathered all the chief priests and the legal experts and asked them where the Christ

was to be born. ⁵They said, "In Bethlehem of Judea, for this is what the prophet wrote:

> ⁶*You, Bethlehem, land of Judah,*
> *by no means are you least among the rulers of Judah,*
> *because from you will come one who governs,*
> *who will shepherd my people Israel.*ᵃ

⁷Then Herod secretly called for the magi and found out from them the time when the star had first appeared. ⁸He sent them to Bethlehem, saying, "Go and search carefully for the child. When you've found him, report to me so that I too may go and honor him." ⁹When they heard the king, they went; and look, the star they had seen in the east went ahead of them until it stood over the place where the child was. ¹⁰When they saw the star, they were filled with joy. ¹¹They entered the house and saw the child with Mary his mother. Falling to their knees, they honored him. Then they opened their treasure chests and presented him with gifts of gold, frankincense, and myrrh. ¹²Because they were warned in a dream not to return to Herod, they went back to their own country by another route.

¹³When the magi had departed, an angel from the Lord appeared to Joseph in a dream and said, "Get up. Take the child and his mother and escape to Egypt. Stay there until I tell you, for Herod will soon search for the child in order to kill him." ¹⁴Joseph got up and, during the night, took the child and his mother to Egypt. ¹⁵He

---

a Micah 5:2; 2 Samuel 5:2

stayed there until Herod died. This fulfilled what the Lord had spoken through the prophet: *I have called my son out of Egypt.*[b]

[16]When Herod knew the magi had fooled him, he grew very angry. He sent soldiers to kill all the children in Bethlehem and in all the surrounding territory who were two years old and younger, according to the time that he had learned from the magi. [17]This fulfilled the word spoken through Jeremiah the prophet:

> [18]*A voice was heard in Ramah,*
> *weeping and much grieving.*
> *Rachel weeping for her children,*
> *and she did not want to be comforted,*
> *because they were no more.*[c]

[19]After King Herod died, an angel from the Lord appeared in a dream to Joseph in Egypt. [20]"Get up," the angel said, "and take the child and his mother and go to the land of Israel. Those who were trying to kill the child are dead." [21]Joseph got up, took the child and his mother, and went to the land of Israel.

INSIGHT AND IDEAS

Yann Martel's *Life of Pi* is the story of a boy who survives at sea after the cargo ship he was traveling on sinks. This treacherous voyage is made all the more difficult by a Bengal tiger named Richard Parker, who also happens to be on his lifeboat.

---

b Hosea 11:1
c Jeremiah 31:15

In the 2012 film adaptation, Pi and his older brother first meet this tiger in their family zoo. Pi foolishly holds out a hunk of meat to the tiger, but his father arrives just in time. As a lesson to the boys, a live goat is tied outside the cage. As they watch, Richard Parker attacks the goat through the bars and drags it away to eat. The message is clear. Tigers eat goats. Lions eat lambs. There is a natural order to this world, and we are not on top.

While stranded together on the lifeboat, Pi and the tiger literally mark their territory. You can see, however, Pi's fear, his hesitation, always watching his back, always waiting for Richard Parker to strike.

In this dog-eat-dog world, we can never be at rest or at peace; we're always trying to stake out our territory or keep ourselves from being eaten. Parents worry about their children. We willingly give up freedoms for a sense of security. We turn away from neighbors because we fear that welcoming them is a threat to our American dream.

In a 2010 segment from *BBC World News* about peace talks between Israel and Palestine, one of the men interviewed said adamantly, "I want peace, but I don't want to surrender." We want the peace that passes all understanding; but we refuse to surrender, we refuse to give in, and we refuse to accept that we are trapped. We are so focused on our own small corner of the world that we cannot see the larger ways in which fear, death, and sin have enslaved us. We are caught in addiction and sinful patterns. The powers of this world beat us down and show us our place. We are limited by systemic sins and stereotypes, prescribed roles, and expectations.

Who is your king? What enslaves you? We might hate the idea of slavery, but think about how often we use images of slavery when talking about love. We talk about being "tied down" to families or jobs, or worse, a spouse referred to as a "ball and chain."

Some of the things that enslave us are good and healthful, but even they can keep us from fullness of life in God. As slaves to the things and people we love, we are trapped in patterns and positions that can consume our lives and control our every action. Like victims who develop Stockholm syndrome, we sometimes have a hard time accepting that we have been captured. We begin to identify with our masters. We defend the patterns that have us trapped. We begin to accept the values of this prison of sin.

The man from Israel failed to realize that he had already surrendered. We all have. We surrender to patriotism and nationalism and consumerism. We surrender to the pressure of family values. We surrender to our jobs and the money they bring. We surrender to expectations and roles that this world has placed upon us. We surrender by accepting a world of sin and evil and "the one who holds the power over death" (Hebrews 2:14).

THE GIFT OF SALVATION

In February 2012, a young man named Trayvon Martin was shot and killed by a neighborhood watch coordinator,

George Zimmerman. Frenzy surrounded the event with cries of racial injustice and criticism of the Florida law "Stand Your Ground." In the end, Zimmerman was acquitted of murder; the jury believed that he acted in self-defense out of fear for his own life.

No matter the details of what happened that night, it was fear that ruled Martin and Zimmerman's actions and ours in the days that followed. Fear of a newcomer or stranger in your community. Fear for your family. Fear of being misunderstood. Fear of being followed. Fear for our life. Those fears are signs of our imprisonment, markers of a life lived under the rule of sin and death. The Sunday after the verdict was announced, the lectionary gospel was the story of the Good Samaritan. What if instead of fear, compassion had ruled the day? What if we could escape our fears? What if we could escape sin and death and live more fully in the peace of Christ?

The longing for the Messiah is the longing for an end to the instinctual fear that entraps us. When Isaiah spoke of one to come, he envisioned a king from the line of David, from the stump of Jesse, who would strike the violent and kill the wicked (Isaiah 11:4).

But rather than a future with lions and lambs ever at war, he describes the peace that will come when "the wolf will live with the lamb, and the leopard will lie down with the young goat; the calf and the young lion will feed together, and a little child will lead them" (Isaiah 11:6).

The magi followed the star to Jerusalem to present the new king with a gift of gold. When they arrived, they found themselves faced with two different ideas of what it meant to be king (Matthew 2:1).

Herod was an appointed ruler who had turned against his fellow Jews. Through political maneuvering, scheming, and treachery, he now sat in Jerusalem as the king of the mountain. Although he was a puppet of the Roman occupiers, Herod would do anything to hold on to his power, going so far as to murder his own sons who posed a threat to his rule. While this king pretends to help the magi, all along, he plots to find the child himself and destroy him (Matthew 2:7-8).

King Herod's reign symbolizes the prison of sin and death. He is trapped by fear and he has enslaved and oppressed others with that fear. Sent to Bethlehem by this king, the magi discover again the star that will lead them to the child. Matthew writes, "When they saw the star, they were filled with joy" (Matthew 2:10).

They were filled with joy.

Maybe they could sense the evil in Herod's heart. Maybe they were relieved that the king they were seeking would not be of his line. Maybe they, too, were longing for liberation and peace.

The gift of gold they brought was a costly precious metal. It symbolized greatness, wealth, and power. In Bethlehem they found not a palace but a small home. Instead of a royal court surrounded by servants, they found a child and his mother. I can imagine that the scene was humbling for the magi from the east. They had brought gold to honor a king and the one they bowed down to worship was not the ruler who sat on the throne in Jerusalem. He was the lowly child born in a manger. The magi never doubted which was the true king.

Jesus is the one we have been waiting for. He has prepared a future where justice reigns. "He will judge the needy with righteousness, and decide with equity for those who suffer in the land" (Isaiah 11:4). Although on earth he didn't wear a golden crown, Christ the King triumphed through the cross and "is now crowned with glory and honor because of the suffering of his death" (Hebrews 2:9b). He assures us, "I was dead, but look! Now I'm alive forever and always. I have the keys of Death and the Grave" (Revelation 1:18).

The gift of salvation is deliverance from fear and death. In Jesus Christ, we find our refuge and the end to the constant turmoil we are trapped within. Although we have been trapped in a prison of sin since the time of Adam and Eve, the Christ child, the babe born in the manger, comes to win our victory and throw open the gates of death (Hebrews 2:14). He has opened the door to everlasting peace and invites us to enter.

OUR RESPONSE

Jesus holds the keys that set us free. Like so many twelve-step programs across the country have helped recovering addicts learn, we simply cannot do it ourselves. We cannot liberate ourselves from this prison, but we know who can. The first three steps of the program echo this gift of salvation:

"We admitted we were powerless over our [sin]—that our lives had become unmanageable."

We "came to believe that a Power greater than ourselves could restore us."

We "made a decision to turn our will and our lives over to the care of God."[1]

What is important is that we need to give our will and our lives to Jesus. Christ the King does not set us free and leave us as masters of our own lives. He sets us free to choose him, to love him, to serve him. Bob Dylan's song "Gotta Serve Somebody" reminds us that we can't escape being slaves. We are always, every day, serving someone or something.

When Jesus broke open the prison of sin and death, he set us free to choose him as our Lord. He is described as "the firstborn from among the dead, and the ruler of the kings of the earth . . . the one who loves us and freed us from our sins by his blood, who made us a kingdom" (Revelation 1:5-6).

---

1 From *http://www.12step.org*.

We have been set free to become members of the reign of Christ our Lord. When we accept this gift of salvation, our allegiance is no longer to sin or fear of death; but we also respond by giving up our allegiance to the things of this earth. We are invited to serve Christ our Lord in complete obedience and become "strangers and immigrants on earth" (Hebrews 11:13).

This means that we cannot draw lines in the sand around our immediate families but must love every child of God like family (Hebrews 13:1). We must let go of our jobs and money as the source of our security and "be content with what [we] have" (Hebrews 13:5). No part of our lives can be set aside and off-limits to God. We are called to fully trust in the one who will never leave or abandon us.

Paul wrote that we can willingly submit ourselves to God's will because we know that God loves us, and because we love God (Romans 6:16-20). Christ is the one who "set free those who were held in slavery their entire lives by their fear of death" (Hebrews 2:15). By taking on our flesh and blood, Jesus entered death itself and made a way through (Hebrews 2:14). When we take refuge in Jesus Christ, we find the king of righteousness and peace who will protect and keep us safe and secure (Hebrews 6:19-7:2).

If you've gotta serve somebody, why not the King of Kings?

In Advent, we wait for Christ to come again to lead us into Zion. Like those who have gone before us, we "are longing for a better country, that is, a heavenly one" (Hebrews 11:16);

but we have found the peace of Christ that enables us to endure. The trials of today are like a refining fire that strips away our fears and helps us to more fully put our lives in God's hands.

Think again about that gift of precious gold. Gold endures, resisting corrosion by air or water. It is the "only metal that loses nothing by contact with fire; indeed the opposite is the case: the quality of gold is enhanced the more it is subjected to fire," wrote Pliny the Elder.[2] As gold is melted, its impurities rise to the surface and the true nature of the substance is revealed.

This gift of salvation is still being given, but we find our peace and strength today because we no longer have to live in fear. Fear led us to push and strain against one another to create our own false sense of security and safety. In Jesus, we find the freedom to be at peace with ourselves and our neighbors, to reach out and to risk relationship, to love with compassion and to fully experience this life, knowing that Jesus has tasted our death and now waits for us as the Lord of life.

---

2 John Healy, *Pliny the Elder on Science and Technology* (New York: Oxford University Press, 1999), page 298.

QUESTIONS

1. Who is the shoot that will grow from the stump of Jesse
(Isaiah 11:1)? What evidence brings you to that conclusion?

2. What will it mean for this person to have the Lord's spirit
resting on him (Isaiah 11:2)? How does this compare to the work
of the Holy Spirit today?

3. What time period or scenario is Isaiah 11 describing? Has this
happened yet?

4. What will a world look like that's filled with the knowledge of
the Lord (Isaiah 11:9)?

5. Why was King Herod troubled by what he heard from the
magi? Why were others troubled as well (Matthew 1:3)?

6. How did the magi have any sort of understanding of the identity of Jesus? Why weren't they warned in a dream not to visit Herod at the beginning?

7. Can you envision any scenarios that might not have led to the deaths of the children in Bethlehem (Matthew 2:16)? Explain your answer.

8. Why is it so difficult to see when we've been enslaved by something or someone? How does Christ free us from slavery?

9. What are some ways fear enslaves people today?

10. Isaiah 11 describes a future where justice reigns. How do you define *justice*? What can you do today to make justice more prevalent?

3

FRANKINCENSE
A GIFT FOR A GOD

SCRIPTURE
HEBREWS 7:18-28; MATTHEW 3:1-12

HEBREWS 7:18-28

[18]On the one hand, an earlier command is set aside because it was weak and useless [19](because the Law made nothing perfect). On the other hand, a better hope is introduced, through which we draw near to God. [20]And this was not done without a solemn pledge! The others have become priests without a solemn pledge, [21]but this priest was affirmed with a solemn pledge by the one who said,

> The Lord has made a solemn pledge
> and will not change his mind:
> You are a priest forever.[a]

---

a Psalm 110:4

²²As a result, Jesus has become the guarantee of a better covenant. ²³The others who became priests are numerous because death prevented them from continuing to serve. ²⁴In contrast, he holds the office of priest permanently because he continues to serve forever. ²⁵This is why he can completely save those who are approaching God through him, because he always lives to speak with God for them.

²⁶It's appropriate for us to have this kind of high priest: holy, innocent, incorrupt, separate from sinners, and raised high above the heavens. ²⁷He doesn't need to offer sacrifices every day like the other high priests, first for their own sins and then for the sins of the people. He did this once for all when he offered himself. ²⁸The Law appoints people who are prone to weakness as high priests, but the content of the solemn pledge, which came after the Law, appointed a Son who has been made perfect forever.

MATTHEW 3:1-12

¹In those days John the Baptist appeared in the desert of Judea announcing, ²"Change your hearts and lives! Here comes the kingdom of heaven!" ³He was the one of whom Isaiah the prophet spoke when he said:

> *The voice of one shouting in the wilderness,*
>   *"Prepare the way for the Lord;*
>   *make his paths straight."*[b]

---

b Isaiah 40:3

⁴John wore clothes made of camel's hair, with a leather belt around his waist. He ate locusts and wild honey.

⁵People from Jerusalem, throughout Judea, and all around the Jordan River came to him. ⁶As they confessed their sins, he baptized them in the Jordan River. ⁷Many Pharisees and Sadducees came to be baptized by John. He said to them, "You children of snakes! Who warned you to escape from the angry judgment that is coming soon? ⁸Produce fruit that shows you have changed your hearts and lives. ⁹And don't even think about saying to yourselves, Abraham is our father. I tell you that God is able to raise up Abraham's children from these stones. ¹⁰The ax is already at the root of the trees. Therefore, every tree that doesn't produce good fruit will be chopped down and tossed into the fire. ¹¹I baptize with water those of you who have changed your hearts and lives. The one who is coming after me is stronger than I am. I'm not worthy to carry his sandals. He will baptize you with the Holy Spirit and with fire. ¹²The shovel he uses to sift the wheat from the husks is in his hands. He will clean out his threshing area and bring the wheat into his barn. But he will burn the husks with a fire that can't be put out."

INSIGHT AND IDEAS

My neighbor's son recently picked up a bad habit—lying. Whether it's a phase or developmental, he has discovered that he can make up stories to try to get away with things. But it hasn't been working. His parents see right through his lies. They catch him all of the time. But they haven't figured out how to get him to stop lying.

In particular, he frequently lies about doing his chores. Once they caught him in a whopper and grounded him for four months. To encourage better behavior, every day he goes without lying he can earn one day back. When he does what he is asked to do, he can earn back more. But each time he is caught lying, another week is added to his "sentence." I think that he might eventually be grounded forever.

The sins we commit have consequences. Other people are harmed by our actions or inactions. We are weighed down with the burden of guilt for what we have done. And our misdeeds are an affront to the God who created us.

In our society, we pay the penalty for societal wrongs through fines, community service, and jail time. We want retribution—a punishment that fits the crime—but we are also seeking restoration. We want to mend relationships or repair the damage done. Ideally, someone who has broken the law will come through the process and be reintegrated into society. My neighbors are hoping that through discipline, their son will learn to stop lying and take responsibility for his actions.

Traditionally, we approach sin in the same way. Sin can be thought of as breaking God's laws; but committing sins also separates us from God. When we sin, we turn our back on our creator.

The Book of Leviticus gave instruction for a Temple sacrifice for each law of God that was broken. For example:

> If you sin: by not providing information after hearing a public solemn pledge even though you are a witness, knowing something, or having seen something so that you become liable to punishment . . . you must confess how you have sinned and bring to the Lord as compensation for the sin that was committed a female from the flock, either a sheep or goat, as a purification offering. The priest will then make reconciliation for you, to remove your sin. (Leviticus 5:1, 5-6)

The offering was intended both as a punishment and as a way to cleanse that sin from your life so that you could be restored to your neighbor and to God.

Cleanliness is important. A person who is ritually unclean is temporarily unsuited to take part in holy activities such as prayer, sacrifice, fasting, and so on. The word *temporarily* is key. A ritual impurity, such as that caused by contact with bodily fluids or menstruation, is not permanent state of being. A ritual washing or an offering makes a person clean again.

Sin itself defiles us, and it defiles God. Anselm of Canterbury, an eleventh-century monk, taught that we could never be saved through these offerings. Like my neighbor kid who might be grounded forever, our sins are compounding with interest; and there is nothing we can do to pay that debt. We owe an infinite debt to God because we have marred God's honor.

The Book of Hebrews describes the laws of God and the sacrificial system as "weak and useless (because the Law made nothing perfect)" (Hebrews 7:18-19). Burnt offerings do not keep us from sinning again and again; sacrifices seek only to restore us to where we were in God's eyes. Hebrews describes the continual need for small realignments rather than an infinite debt. The system is imperfect, the priests and pastors are flawed, and we will forever be trapped in a cycle of sin and reconciliation. That is not good enough in God's eyes.

God does not want burnt offerings and sacrifices. When our lives are filled with sin, good deeds mean nothing. They can't earn us a place in God's heart. In fact, the hypocrisy of them serves only to anger our Lord because they cover up the truth: We need to be washed clean. We need to be transformed from the inside out.

THE GIFT OF SALVATION

In Matthew and Mark's Gospels, a strange man named John called people to repentance. He set up camp by the Jordan River, and people were so moved by his words that they came to him from everywhere. They were yearning for a chance to let go of their pasts, to confess their sins, and to be made clean.

The people who journeyed into the wilderness were moved by this tangible act of letting themselves be washed by the waters of the Jordan. As the cold water drifted past them, the current symbolically took their sins away.

But even John the Baptizer that knew that this was only the beginning. He knew that this act of repentance wasn't enough. It wasn't enough to say, "I'm sorry." You actually needed to live differently. Water wasn't enough. Sacrifice wasn't enough.

So John proclaimed that one was coming who would baptize with the Holy Spirit and with fire. One was coming who would not only forgive but would set things right. And one day, by the banks of the Jordan, Jesus appeared.

Jesus went into the waters not because he needed to repent, not because he was unclean, but for us. He entered the water for the same reason that he went to the cross—so that we might be saved. Through the gift of salvation, we are made holy by the power of Jesus Christ and the Holy Spirit enters our life. Jesus came not to merely offer forgiveness but to actually make us holy. He brings to us a new covenant, written on our hearts, a promise that lasts forever.

While the magi sought the King of the Jews, they also brought with them a gift fit for a god: frankincense, the resin of a particular tree. When frankincense is burned on an altar during a sacrifice or ritual, the fragrance rises up to God like prayer. The magi's gift showed that they came not only to honor a king but also to worship a god. Jesus might be fully human, but we also confess that he is fully divine. While the child is like us, he is also completely different.

Traditionally, the Temple was served by the Levitical priests, a tribe of Israel set apart for this purpose. Like the priests and pastors of today, they were not perfect. They were just people. Their time of service came and went with the seasons of their lives. Before they could offer the sacrifices for the people, they, too, needed to be cleansed from their sins. Jesus came as our priest, but Hebrews assures us that he was a priest like no other in Israel:

> He holds the office of priest permanently because he
> continues to serve forever . . . holy, innocent, incorrupt,
> separate from sinners, and raised high above the heavens.
> He doesn't need to offer sacrifices every day like the other
> high priests, first for their own sins and then for the sins of
> the people. He did this once for all when he offered himself
> (Hebrews 7:24, 26-27).

What came before with the Temple and the priests were
mere shadows of what God was preparing to do for us in
Jesus Christ (Hebrews 8:5). And in the Protestant tradition,
the sacraments of Communion and baptism are shadows
too. Through the mystery of God, they symbolize the gift of
salvation, washing us clean and paying the penalty for our
sin. As a pastor, I am acutely aware that it is not my power
that blesses the bread and the cup and the water but God's.
Through these mighty acts of salvation, we are not offering
new sacrifices but are participating in what Jesus Christ has
already done.

OUR RESPONSE

Last summer, I had a day when all of the ugly seemed to
seep out of me. I was grumpy and snarky. I was full of
gossip and downright rude to others. While no excuse,
my husband and I had a fight the night before and the
disagreement had not been resolved. The anger and
frustration I was feeling crept out in a thousand different
ways. And as luck would have it, we were having a big
family get-together that day with my in-laws.

My husband's grandfather is one of those strong and silent guys who don't really speak unless it's important. He noticed my attitude, and he said something. Now, I am not a perfect person, and I will never pretend to be a perfect person. But as soon as he confronted me, I realized just how far I was from perfect on that day.

My husband and I had had an argument, but I let the anger have control. I took all of those feelings and set them aside in a neat little box and decided that I didn't need God's help in dealing with them. I gave that anger power. I gave it free rein. I was bitter and had a quick wit and biting humor; and when I washed the dishes, I banged pots and pans around. I was a terrible person that day.

I *chose* to let sin in. Even though I have been set free from the power of sin and death and have been washed clean through the blood of Jesus Christ, I let sin in. Even though I had been made holy, I let sin trip me up.

As the people of God, we are invited to accept the gift of salvation and to honor it. Unlike the sacrificial system, where the pattern was to sin, wash, and repeat, the sacrifice of Jesus Christ makes us holy. Through the one perfect sacrifice, our High Priest invites us to quit sin cold turkey. No turning back. No nicotine patches.

When we accept the gift of salvation, the Law is no longer a burden. It is written on our hearts and transformed by his sacrifice; living God's will is a joy. Like a dry land that has been filled with refreshing water, our lives of sin have been washed clean. The fruit of salvation blossoms in our lives with abundance and singing.

Living without sin is not easy, because we have been living with it for so long. But like water springing forth in the desert, the impossible becomes real through the saving power of God. We can quit our lives of sin cold turkey by urging one another on in the promises of God. With Isaiah, we raise our voices, "Strengthen the weak hands, and support the unsteady knees. Say to those who are panicking: 'Be strong! Don't fear!'" (Isaiah 35:3-4; Hebrews 12:12).

Like the magi's gift of frankincense, we place our lives into the hands of Jesus Christ. Together we find the strength to shout no when sin comes along. When violence breaks out, we can resist. When darkness rears its ugly head, we hold fast to the light. As Hebrews 12 reminds us, we "have such a great cloud of witnesses surrounding us. Let's throw off any extra baggage, get rid of the sin that trips us up, and fix our eyes on Jesus, faith's pioneer and perfecter" (Hebrews 12:1-2a).

The sacraments of Communion and baptism and the worship of the community of faith remind us of what Jesus Christ has done. They fill us with the power of the Holy Spirit so that we can remember. With joy, we join with others at the table and the font to sing God's praises.

QUESTIONS

1. In what ways was the Law insufficient (Hebrews 7:18)? How is Jesus the guarantee of a better covenant? (Hebrews 7:22)

2. Compare and contrast Jesus to the priests of the old covenant.

3. How did Jesus change the Old Testament system of sacrifices for sins? Why was he able to do this (Hebrews 7:26-28)?

4. What does it mean to change one's heart and life (Matthew 3:2)? What does *hearts* mean in this passage?

5. What is the fruit John speaks of in Matthew 3:8? How do we know whether we're producing the right kind of fruit?

6. How did John the Baptizer know so much about what Jesus would do? How should we handle the harsh language John uses?

7. What is sin? How does it defile us?

8. What is the connection between baptism, Communion, and the sacrifice Jesus made on the cross? Why are the sacraments of Communion and baptism so important?

9. Considering that we've been made clean through Christ's perfect sacrifice, why is it still so easy to get tripped up in sin?

10. Is it really possible to quit sin cold turkey? What are your experiences in attempting to overcome the power of sin?

4

MYRRH
A GIFT FOR A PROPHET

SCRIPTURE
MATTHEW 1:18-25; HEBREWS 5:7-10; 11:32-40

MATTHEW 1:18-25

[18]This is how the birth of Jesus Christ took place. When Mary his mother was engaged to Joseph, before they were married, she became pregnant by the Holy Spirit. [19]Joseph her husband was a righteous man. Because he didn't want to humiliate her, he decided to call off their engagement quietly. [20]As he was thinking about this, an angel from the Lord appeared to him in a dream and said, "Joseph son of David, don't be afraid to take Mary as your wife, because the child she carries was conceived by the Holy Spirit. [21]She will give birth to a son, and you will call him Jesus, because he will save his people from their sins." [22]Now all of this took place so that what the Lord had spoken through the prophet would be fulfilled:

[23]*Look! A virgin will become pregnant and give birth to a son,
And they will call him,* Emmanuel.[a]

(*Emmanuel* means "God with us.")

[24]When Joseph woke up, he did just as an angel from God
commanded and took Mary as his wife. [25]But he didn't have
sexual relations with her until she gave birth to a son. Joseph
called him Jesus.

HEBREWS 5:7-10

[7]During his days on earth, Christ offered prayers and requests
with loud cries and tears as his sacrifices to the one who was
able to save him from death. He was heard because of his godly
devotion. [8]Although he was a Son, he learned obedience from
what he suffered. [9]After he had been made perfect, he became
the source of eternal salvation for everyone who obeys him. [10]He
was appointed by God to be a high priest according to the order
of Melchizedek.

HEBREWS 11:32-40

[32]What more can I say? I would run out of time if I told you
about Gideon, Barak, Samson, Jephthah, David, Samuel, and the
prophets. [33]Through faith they conquered kingdoms, brought
about justice, realized promises, shut the mouths of lions, [34]put
out raging fires, escaped from the edge of the sword, found

---

a Isaiah 7:14

strength in weakness, were mighty in war, and routed foreign armies. [35]Women received back their dead by resurrection. Others were tortured and refused to be released so they could gain a better resurrection.

[36]But others experienced public shame by being taunted and whipped; they were even put in chains and in prison. [37]They were stoned to death, they were cut in two, and they died by being murdered with swords. They went around wearing the skins of sheep and goats, needy, oppressed, and mistreated. [38]The world didn't deserve them. They wandered around in deserts, mountains, caves, and holes in the ground.

[39]All these people didn't receive what was promised, though they were given approval for their faith. [40]God provided something better for us so they wouldn't be made perfect without us.

INSIGHT AND IDEAS

During the Season Six finale of *House*, a woman is trapped in a building by an explosion. As they work to get her out, Dr. House is by her side. Hanna's condition is bleak and other personnel have been evacuated because the structure is unstable, but House refuses to leave. In her desperation, she turns to him and asks him to pray with her.

House is not a man of faith. He thinks that religion is superstitious nonsense and frequently butts heads with colleagues and patients over God. So his first response is a resolute, "No." He doesn't believe in God. Hanna answers, "Neither do I."

In that foxhole, the two sit for a few moments in silence, joining in a moment of silent prayer to a God neither believes exists. As the moment passes, Hanna confesses that she believed that if she was good—if she tried to do the right thing—everything would be OK. But here she is, stuck underneath a building. Why do these things happen?

When the magi arrive at the palace in Jerusalem, they discover the tyrant Herod, who, full of scheming, shares with them the prophecy about a messiah from Bethlehem. He says, "When you've found him, report to me so that I too may go and honor him" (Matthew 2:7-8). They leave and days pass by. Herod grows anxious, not to find the child and give up his hard earned power, but so that he can end the threat against his rule. When the magi don't return, Herod is driven to the brink with insecurity and sends troops to the quiet town of Bethlehem to kill every boy under the age of two. He takes no chances (Matthew 2:16-18).

We know that God intervened and warned the magi not to return. We know that an angel warned Joseph of the threat and that the family escaped the terror Herod afflicted on the countryside. They were so afraid that they lived in exile in Egypt until long after Herod's death (Matthew 2:12-13, 19). But what always bothers me about this story are the other children—the innocent babies who were killed. What about the mothers who cried out in Bethlehem?

All around us are institutions of oppression. Injustice
abounds. Cancer and illness take our loved ones before
their time. more than half a million children die every year
from preventable, treatable diseases. The disparity between
the rich and poor grows daily. We live in a world filled with
pain, terror, and despair. Trying to make sense of it all, we
struggle with why bad things happen to good people. If
God is so good, why does evil exist? Why is this happening
to me?

Maybe instead of asking *why,* we need to be asking *where*:
Where is God in the midst of our suffering?

THE GIFT OF SALVATION

In 2009, I heard theologian Jürgen Moltmann talk about
how he came to know Christ. He was born into a secular
family in the 1920s, with no connection to the church. As a
young man, he remembers with horror the "firestorm" that
destroyed much of his hometown, Hamburg, killing more
than 40,000 people. A person standing next to him died
while he was inexplicably spared.

At eighteen, he was drafted to the German army and almost
immediately surrendered to Allied forces. In prison camps,
he began to comprehend what his people had done. He was
overcome with the shame of his culture and the grief of losing
so many loved ones. He had watched close friends die and
learned about the extermination of the Jews, but he could
not begin to express his loss. The humanism and education
of his youth could not account for what he had witnessed.

Given a Bible by an American chaplain, he found the words he was seeking: *forsakenness, destruction, lament.* He found solidarity in the words of the psalmist, echoed by Jesus: "My God! My God, why have you left me all alone? Why are you so far from saving me—so far from my anguished groans?" (Psalm 22:1). He found a "fellow sufferer who understood."

When he was moved to a new camp, Moltmann was surprised by the compassion of Scottish guards. They looked at him and his fellow Germans as human beings, and he felt forgiveness without even having to confess.

We can ask the "why" question all we want. We can ask why Moltmann lived and his friends died. We can ask why Hitler and his armies killed so many. But no answer to those questions will help us find peace. However, if we ask the "where" question, we can find consolation. Where is God in our suffering?

God is with us. God is beside us. The Son of God, Emmanuel, God with us. Our whole creation groans for salvation (Romans 8:22) and into this fallen, broken world God comes. Natural disasters, accidents, illness, oppression—all of these are signs that the world is not as it should be, but God so loves the world (John 3:16-17) that in Jesus Christ, our loving and compassionate God is willing to taste death for us all (Hebrews 2:9). Born to Mary, through the power of the Holy Spirit (Matthew 1:18, 23), Jesus was born to suffer.

The final gift of the magi, the gift of myrrh, reminds us that the king and the priest was also the prophet, the suffering Word of God, the one who embodied the very character of God.

The prophets of God have done ridiculous things to demonstrate God's love, anger, and justice. Ezekiel lay on his side for more than a year to symbolize the years of sin of the people (Ezekiel 4:4). Jeremiah bought a field to symbolize the promise of redemption even in the midst of destruction (Jeremiah 32). Hosea married a prostitute to show how God remains faithful even when we are not (Hosea 1). Their lives were not easy because their actions were as important as their words. Many were driven out into the wilderness, unwelcome, rejected for the harsh words of truth God set on their hearts.

The gift of myrrh represents the death and sorrow that would come. Myrrh was offered to Jesus as he was crucified (Mark 15:23); it was mixed with the spices that Nicodemus brought to anoint his dead body (John 19:39). In Jesus' actions, like those of the prophets, we see the truth about how God loves us. Our savior suffers with us, crucified, bloody, and beaten. He speaks truth to rulers such as Pilate. He eats with sinners. He loves those whom society has turned away, even when it leads the powers-that-be to destroy him. When Jesus goes to that cross, it is not only for the guilty; he also suffers with us.

But Jesus doesn't suffer for the sake of suffering. He suffers so that we see how we have been oppressors. He suffers to help us hear the voices of victims. He suffers to reconcile us to one another. "He endured the cross, ignoring the shame, for the sake of the joy that was laid out in front of him" (Hebrews 12:2). The joy laid out before us is the other side of the cross. Our suffering God is also a resurrecting God. As he suffers with victims, he promises justice. As he dies with us and grieves with us, he leads the way to healing and resurrection. Death does not have the final say. This creation will not perish because our God is making all things new. Love wins.

We long for the day of the Lord, but it's not fully here. It's not whole yet. We are still living in a fallen, broken, messed-up creation. And so in our midst, Jesus comes to walk beside us, to suffer with us, and to show us a glimpse of the promised resurrection life.

OUR RESPONSE

One afternoon, Amy walked into my church and asked to use the telephone. She had just been released from the county jail and was far from home, but no one had come to pick her up. "Not a problem," I said. And while she sat in the office, dialing numbers and getting no response, I picked out the hymns for Sunday. When she finally got hold of someone, her"friend," the friend chewed her out; so Amy hung up in frustration. "Are you stranded?" I asked.

Amy was seven months pregnant and needed to get home, so I offered her a ride. During the hour-and-a-half-long trip, we talked and stopped for a meal. She was able to get a bit of rest before we made it to her home. An outsider might see a random act of kindness done to a stranger, but disciples of Christ understand that it was far from a random act and she was far from a stranger. We have experienced the presence of God in our times of trial ,and we respond by being with others in theirs.

Faced with the suffering of this world, Jürgen Moltmann said that we need to hasten the coming of the Lord. Rather than adjusting to unjust conditions in the present, we who know that things can and will be changed must resist conformity and silence. We must take up our crosses and follow. It is not enough to wait for the day of resurrection. The gift of salvation sets us free to live in that reality today, as those who "saw the promises from a distance and welcomed them" (Hebrews 11:13).

Jesus invites us to follow him into suffering. We are called to take up the cross of empathy and suffer with our neighbors. We are called to take up the cross of healing, to sit with those who are sick, and to grieve with their loved ones. We are called to take up the cross of forgiveness, go to the prison, and love our enemies. To do so, we need to see every person with love.

The Hebrew word for *kindness*, *khesed*, describes how we behave when we have a deep commitment to another person. As people of faith, our obligations go further than our families or neighbors. We are children of God, and we must love whomever God loves. God is for us, so we must be for others. The Book of Hebrews tells of the faithful who exemplify this prophetic life. They stood in solidarity with the oppressed, risked their lives to fight injustice, and spoke truth to those in power. While some were victorious, many suffered greatly for their Lord (Hebrews 11:1-40). How did they do it? How do we take up our crosses to follow?

Entering into suffering is not easy. Think about how Joseph responded when he discovered his fiancée, Mary, was pregnant. Can you imagine how incomprehensible the story of "Holy Spirit conception" must have been? He was "a righteous man," implying that the right thing to do was to walk away, to leave her so that neither of them would be humiliated by the pregnancy. But then an angel of the Lord intervened: "Don't be afraid to take Mary as your wife. . . . She will give birth to a son, and you will call him Jesus" (Matthew 1:20-21).

Like Joseph, we are called to enter difficult situations in love rather than to walk away. We are to be in solidarity with those who are suffering. The love of Christ gives us the strength to endure, to stand our ground, and to sympathize without fear. "We aren't the sort of people who timidly draw back and end up being destroyed. We're the sort of people who have faith so that our whole beings are preserved" (Hebrews 10:39). We know that Emmanuel, God with us, joined in our suffering because he loved us.

When Amy walked into my office, I was called to love. I could get her home. I could stop what I was doing and have lunch with her. I could let her know that it didn't matter whether she had come from prison, or the hospital, or the church. She was loved.

QUESTIONS

1. Why were Mary and Joseph put in such a potentially controversial and embarrassing position (Matthew 1:18)?

2. What does it mean that Joseph was a "righteous" man? Why did he decide to call off the engagement to Mary (Matthew 1:19)?

3. How did the angel from the Lord appear to Joseph? Why would an angel appear in this way (Matthew 1:20)?

4. What is significant about the name *Jesus* (Matthew 1:21)?

5. How does Jesus serve as a priest for the ones who believe in him (Hebrews 5:7-10)? What does it mean to be a high priest according to the order of Melchizedek?

6. What is the connection between faith and suffering? What does it mean to be "given approval" for one's faith (Hebrews 11:39)?

7. Why is it comforting to know that God is with us when we suffer? What does suffering accomplish? Is it wrong to pray to avoid suffering?

8. Considering the fact that we still live in a broken world, how do we live in the reality of the kingdom of God today (Hebrews 11:13)?

9. How do we cultivate love for those beyond the circle of our family and friends?

10. What are some practical ways to follow Christ into suffering? What does this mean for a twenty-first-century Christian?

CPSIA information can be obtained at www.ICGtesting.com
Printed in the USA
BVOW09s2007071014

369831BV00006B/29/P